the book of good

a journal to help you
find the good in each day

Sometimes it can be hard to find the good in each day. But it's out there—you just have to teach yourself how to find it.

This journal is for those looking for a way to stop negativity from dominating your thoughts. All you have to do is write three good things that happened each day—no matter how small or inconsequential they feel.

Each day, write three good things, and after a few weeks, it'll start to get easier. Will it turn the world into rainbows and puppies?

No.

But isn't it worth trying?

THE BOOK OF GOOD: NATURE

Copyright © 2019 by Left-Handed Mitten Publications, LLC
All rights reserved. No part of this book may be reproduced in any form or by any electronic or mechanical means, including informational storage and retrieval systems, without permission in writing from Left-Handed Mitten Publications except by a reviewer who may quote brief passages in a review.

Published by Left-Handed Mitten Publications
ISBN-13: 978-1-0878-4087-1
UPC

Writing, book design, and formatting by Melanie Hooyenga.
Website: melaniehoo.com
Email: melaniehooyenga@gmail.com
Newsletter: melaniehoo.com/hoos-letter
Twitter & Instagram: @melaniehoo
Facebook: MelanieHooyenga
PO Box 554, Grand Haven, MI 49417

Cover design by Adrienne Whisman.
Website: awanderingnomad.com

the book of good

Left-Handed Mitten
Publications

This journal belongs to

_____

_____

_____

week 1 _____

Sunday _____

_____

_____

Monday _____

_____

_____

Tuesday _____

_____

_____

Wednesday _____

_____

_____

Thursday

Friday

Saturday

Three best things this week

week 2 _____

Sunday _____
_____
_____

Monday _____
_____
_____

Tuesday _____
_____
_____

Wednesday _____
_____
_____

Thursday _____

_____

_____

Friday _____

_____

_____

Saturday _____

_____

_____

Three best things this week

_____

_____

_____

week 3 _____

Sunday _____
_____
_____

Monday _____
_____
_____

Tuesday _____
_____
_____

Wednesday _____
_____
_____

Thursday _____

_____

_____

Friday _____

_____

_____

Saturday _____

_____

_____

Three best things this week

_____

_____

_____

week 4 _____

Sunday _____

_____

_____

Monday _____

_____

_____

Tuesday _____

_____

_____

Wednesday _____

_____

_____

Thursday _____

_____

_____

Friday _____

_____

_____

Saturday _____

_____

_____

Three best things this week

_____

_____

_____

week 5 _____

Sunday _____
_____
_____

Monday _____
_____
_____

Tuesday _____
_____
_____

Wednesday _____
_____
_____

Thursday

Friday

Saturday

Three best things this week

week 6 _____

Sunday _____
_____
_____

Monday _____
_____
_____

Tuesday _____
_____
_____

Wednesday _____
_____
_____

Thursday _____

_____

_____

Friday _____

_____

_____

Saturday _____

_____

_____

Three best things this week

_____

_____

_____

week 7 _____

Sunday _____
_____
_____

Monday _____
_____
_____

Tuesday _____
_____
_____

Wednesday _____
_____
_____

Thursday _____

Friday _____

Saturday _____

Three best things this week

week 8 _____

Sunday _____

_____

_____

Monday _____

_____

_____

Tuesday _____

_____

_____

Wednesday _____

_____

_____

Thursday

Friday

Saturday

Three best things this week

week 9 _____

Sunday _____
_____
_____

Monday _____
_____
_____

Tuesday _____
_____
_____

Wednesday _____
_____
_____

Thursday

Friday

Saturday

Three best things this week

week 10

Sunday

Monday

Tuesday

Wednesday

Thursday _____

_____

_____

Friday _____

_____

_____

Saturday _____

_____

_____

Three best things this week

_____

_____

_____

week 11

Sunday

Monday

Tuesday

Wednesday

Thursday _____

_____

_____

Friday _____

_____

_____

Saturday _____

_____

_____

Three best things this week

_____

_____

_____

week 12 _____

Sunday _____
_____
_____

Monday _____
_____
_____

Tuesday _____
_____
_____

Wednesday _____
_____
_____

Thursday _____

_____

_____

Friday _____

_____

_____

Saturday _____

_____

_____

Three best things this week

_____

_____

_____

week 13

Sunday

Monday

Tuesday

Wednesday

Thursday _____

_____

_____

Friday _____

_____

_____

Saturday _____

_____

_____

Three best things this week

_____

_____

_____

You've made it past the first few months! By now, coming up with three good things should be feeling more natural.

Take a moment to reflect on any changes in your thinking, or your general outlook on the world.

week 14

Sunday

Monday

Tuesday

Wednesday

Thursday _____

_____

_____

Friday _____

_____

_____

Saturday _____

_____

_____

Three best things this week

_____

_____

_____

week 15 _____

Sunday _____

Monday _____

Tuesday _____

Wednesday _____

Thursday _____

Friday _____

Saturday _____

Three best things this week

week 16

Sunday

Monday

Tuesday

Wednesday

Thursday

Friday

Saturday

Three best things this week

week 17

Sunday

Monday

Tuesday

Wednesday

Thursday

Friday

Saturday

Three best things this week

week 18

Sunday

Monday

Tuesday

Wednesday

Thursday

Friday

Saturday

Three best things this week

week 19

Sunday

Monday

Tuesday

Wednesday

Thursday

Friday

Saturday

Three best things this week

week 20

Sunday

Monday

Tuesday

Wednesday

Thursday

Friday

Saturday

Three best things this week

week 21

Sunday

Monday

Tuesday

Wednesday

Thursday ___

___
___

Friday ___

___
___

Saturday ___

___
___

Three best things this week

___
___
___

week 22

Sunday

Monday

Tuesday

Wednesday

Thursday _____

_____

_____

Friday _____

_____

_____

Saturday _____

_____

_____

Three best things this week

_____

_____

_____

week 23 _____

Sunday _____
_____
_____

Monday _____
_____
_____

Tuesday _____
_____
_____

Wednesday _____
_____
_____

Thursday

Friday

Saturday

Three best things this week

week 24 _____

Sunday _____

Monday _____

Tuesday _____

Wednesday _____

Thursday _____

_____

_____

Friday _____

_____

_____

Saturday _____

_____

_____

Three best things this week

_____

_____

_____

week 25

Sunday

Monday

Tuesday

Wednesday

Thursday _____

_____

_____

Friday _____

_____

_____

Saturday _____

_____

_____

Three best things this week

_____

_____

_____

week 26

Sunday

Monday

Tuesday

Wednesday

Thursday _____

_____

_____

Friday _____

_____

_____

Saturday _____

_____

_____

Three best things this week

_____

_____

_____

You're halfway there! Your three good things should be a habit by now, and you might catch yourself noting good things as they happen so you can write them down later.

Take a moment to reflect on any changes in your thinking, or your general outlook on the world.

week 27 _____

Sunday _____
_____
_____

Monday _____
_____
_____

Tuesday _____
_____
_____

Wednesday _____
_____
_____

Thursday _____

_____

_____

Friday _____

_____

_____

Saturday _____

_____

_____

Three best things this week

_____

_____

_____

week 28

Sunday

Monday

Tuesday

Wednesday

Thursday _____

_____

_____

Friday _____

_____

_____

Saturday _____

_____

_____

Three best things this week

_____

_____

_____

week 29

Sunday

Monday

Tuesday

Wednesday

Thursday _____

_____

_____

Friday _____

_____

_____

Saturday _____

_____

_____

Three best things this week

_____

_____

_____

week 30

Sunday

Monday

Tuesday

Wednesday

Thursday _____

Friday _____

Saturday _____

Three best things this week

week 31

Sunday

Monday

Tuesday

Wednesday

Thursday _____

Friday _____

Saturday _____

Three best things this week

week 32

Sunday

Monday

Tuesday

Wednesday

Thursday

Friday

Saturday

Three best things this week

week 33

Sunday

Monday

Tuesday

Wednesday

Thursday _____

_____

_____

Friday _____

_____

_____

Saturday _____

_____

_____

Three best things this week

_____

_____

_____

week 34

Sunday

Monday

Tuesday

Wednesday

Thursday _____

_____

_____

Friday _____

_____

_____

Saturday _____

_____

_____

Three best things this week

_____

_____

_____

week 35

Sunday

Monday

Tuesday

Wednesday

Thursday

Friday

Saturday

Three best things this week

week 36

Sunday

Monday

Tuesday

Wednesday

Thursday _____

_____

_____

Friday _____

_____

_____

Saturday _____

_____

_____

Three best things this week

_____

_____

_____

week 37

Sunday

Monday

Tuesday

Wednesday

Thursday

Friday

Saturday

Three best things this week

week 38

Sunday

Monday

Tuesday

Wednesday

Thursday

Friday

Saturday

Three best things this week

week 39

Sunday

Monday

Tuesday

Wednesday

Thursday

Friday

Saturday

Three best things this week

Did you ever think you'd make it three-quarters of the year? Writing three good things each day is just part of what you do now, so go ahead and take a moment to reflect on any changes in your thinking, or your general outlook on the world.

week 40

Sunday

Monday

Tuesday

Wednesday

Thursday ___

Friday ___

Saturday ___

Three best things this week

week 41

Sunday

Monday

Tuesday

Wednesday

Thursday _____

_____

_____

Friday _____

_____

_____

Saturday _____

_____

_____

Three best things this week

_____

_____

_____

week 42

Sunday

Monday

Tuesday

Wednesday

Thursday

Friday

Saturday

Three best things this week

week 43

Sunday

Monday

Tuesday

Wednesday

Thursday _____

_____

_____

Friday _____

_____

_____

Saturday _____

_____

_____

Three best things this week

_____

_____

_____

week 44

Sunday

Monday

Tuesday

Wednesday

Thursday _____

_____

_____

Friday _____

_____

_____

Saturday _____

_____

_____

Three best things this week

_____

_____

_____

week 45

Sunday

Monday

Tuesday

Wednesday

Thursday ___

Friday ___

Saturday ___

Three best things this week

week 46 _____

Sunday _____

Monday _____

Tuesday _____

Wednesday _____

Thursday

Friday

Saturday

Three best things this week

week 47

Sunday

Monday

Tuesday

Wednesday

Thursday ___

Friday ___

Saturday ___

Three best things this week

week 48 _____

Sunday _____
_____
_____

Monday _____
_____
_____

Tuesday _____
_____
_____

Wednesday _____
_____
_____

Thursday _____

_____

_____

Friday _____

_____

_____

Saturday _____

_____

_____

Three best things this week

_____

_____

_____

week 49

Sunday

Monday

Tuesday

Wednesday

Thursday

Friday

Saturday

Three best things this week

week 50

Sunday

Monday

Tuesday

Wednesday

Thursday _____

Friday _____

Saturday _____

Three best things this week

week 51 _____

Sunday _____
_____
_____

Monday _____
_____
_____

Tuesday _____
_____
_____

Wednesday _____
_____
_____

Thursday _____

_____

_____

Friday _____

_____

_____

Saturday _____

_____

_____

Three best things this week

_____

_____

_____

week 52 _____

Sunday _____
_____
_____

Monday _____
_____
_____

Tuesday _____
_____
_____

Wednesday _____
_____
_____

Thursday _____

_____

_____

Friday _____

_____

_____

Saturday _____

_____

_____

Three best things this week

_____

_____

_____

Congratulations, you made it!

Hopefully you've reached a point where the good in each day is no longer elusive. Where hope lingers longer than despair. Where the world has turned into rainbow and puppies.

On this last page, take a moment to write down three things that stood out this year. Something that changed your outlook, or made you realize that there is good in the world if you just take a moment to pay attention.

Or write more than that. You've earned it.

www.ingramcontent.com/pod-product-compliance
Lightning Source LLC
Chambersburg PA
CBHW030451010526
44118CB00011B/884